T0165015

Winning Your B.C. Injury Claim: How to successfully navigate the ICBC minefield

By
Chris Temple, LL.B.

Order this book online at www.trafford.com/08-0740
or email orders@trafford.com

Most Trafford titles are also available at major online book retailers.

© Copyright 2008, 2010 Christopher Temple.
All rights reserved. No part of this publication may be reproduced, stored in a retrieval system, or
transmitted, in any form or by any means, electronic, mechanical, photocopying, recording, or
otherwise, without the written prior permission of the author.

Note for Librarians: A cataloguing record for this book is available from Library
and Archives Canada at www.collectionscanada.ca/amicus/index-e.html

Printed in Victoria, BC, Canada.

ISBN: 978-1-4251-8043-0 (sc)

*We at Trafford believe that it is the responsibility of us all, as both individuals
and corporations, to make choices that are environmentally and socially sound.
You, in turn, are supporting this responsible conduct each time you purchase a
Trafford book, or make use of our publishing services. To find out how you are
helping, please visit www.trafford.com/responsiblepublishing.html*

*Our mission is to efficiently provide the world's finest, most comprehensive
book publishing service, enabling every author to experience success.
To find out how to publish your book, your way, and have it available
worldwide, visit us online at www.trafford.com/10510*

www.trafford.com

North America & international
toll-free: 1 888 232 4444 (USA & Canada)
phone: 250 383 6864 ♦ fax: 250 383 6804
email: info@trafford.com

The United Kingdom & Europe
phone: +44 (0)1865 722 113 ♦ local rate: 0845 230 9601
facsimile: +44 (0)1865 722 868 ♦ email: info.uk@trafford.com

10 9 8 7 6 5 4

TABLE OF CONTENTS:

Introduction

If you have been injured in an accident, obtaining this book will be one of the best decisions you make regarding your injury claim.

My name is Chris Temple. For more than twenty-five years I have legally represented individuals with accident, injury or disability claims in British Columbia against insurance companies. Most of my cases are referred to me by former clients, medical people, and other lawyers.

I wrote *Winning Your BC Injury Claim: How to Successfully Navigate the ICBC Minefield* to give you good, solid information *before* you hire a lawyer or deal with ICBC so you can obtain fair compensation for your injury claim. Even if you don't need a lawyer to represent you in your claim, you should be armed with this important information right at the beginning - *before* an ICBC adjuster tries to persuade you to visit a doctor of its choosing or to settle your case before you have recovered. Most lawyers will require you to make an appointment to get some of the information I provide in this book, but I would rather you be informed *today*. I believe you should have access to this information right now, without any pressure, so you don't fall victim to insurance companies or to lawyer advertising.

In the book, I discuss the most common and important questions people have asked me over the years on various subjects regarding their injury claims. I follow each question with a straightforward, easy-to-read answer. If you have further questions, you may contact me without obligation. For more information about me, please visit www.icbcinjurylawyers.ca.

If you're like me, you do your homework before making an important decision. And you do have important decisions to make. At some point you must decide how you want to pursue your accident case. Do you hire a lawyer or go it alone? If you go it alone, how do you deal with the ICBC adjuster? What information is important? What potential landmines lie ahead? If you're thinking about hiring a lawyer, my book will help you search for an experienced and qualified personal injury lawyer.

It is not my intention to give legal advice in this book. I can offer suggestions and identify traps, but please do not construe anything you read in this book as legal advice until you have agreed to hire me as your lawyer *and* I have agreed, in writing, to accept your case.

I wish you every success in fully recovering from your injuries, obtaining the best possible medical care, and receiving fair compensation for all the pain, suffering and other losses and challenges you will unfortunately experience because of your accident.

Chris R. Temple
June 2008

CHAPTER 1

THE 12 BIGGEST MISTAKES TO AVOID WHEN MAKING AN ICBC CLAIM

Over the years I have compiled a list of the twelve biggest mistakes that can harm your ICBC accident case. These mistakes are based on my extensive experience handling accident claims as well as on my discussions with colleagues. The twelve biggest mistakes are as follows:

1. You are not prepared for your first meeting with an ICBC adjuster.
Before you see an ICBC adjuster, contact the office of your doctor, physiotherapist or chiropractor to confirm the dates that you received related treatment before the accident. This will ensure that you do not misstate your previous medical problems in the statement the adjuster will prepare and ask you to sign.

If you think you may be partly at fault for the accident, speak to a lawyer immediately so he or she can prepare you for your interview with the ICBC adjuster. Failure to do this could severely jeopardize your claim. See Chapter 2.

2. Your doctor does not examine you regularly after your accident.
It is extremely important that your doctor examine you at least once per month during your period of significant pain. See Chapter 17.

3. After your accident, you are examined by a series of doctors in a walk-in clinic.
Try to find a family doctor. If you can't find one, choose one doctor at a walk-in clinic and see only that doctor. Check to see what shifts that doctor works.

4. When you attend an ICBC-appointed doctor, you do not see your own medical specialist.
ICBC uses the same medical specialists all the time. The report from such a specialist may well harm your claim. You won't know this because ICBC will not give it to you. Seek legal advice if ICBC asks you to see its chosen specialist. See Chapter 18.

5. You agree with ICBC to an excessive reduction of your past wage loss claim from gross to net.
ICBC will often claim a deduction of 30% to arrive at net; however, this deduction should usually be much less. Agree to only a small deduction for income tax and EI premiums. See Chapter 15.

6. You do not get all the treatment you need.
ICBC often stops funding treatment even though your doctor thinks this would be beneficial. Consider talking to a lawyer about alternative ways to fund the treatment your doctor thinks you need.

7. ICBC does not reimburse you monthly for your physiotherapist or chiropractor user fees.
ICBC frequently reimburses user fees monthly. Insist that your adjuster do this for you. See Chapter 2.

8. You do not obtain the household help you need.
If your doctor documents that you are unable to do most of your household chores, ICBC is required to fund up to $145 per week for household assistance.

If your doctor thinks that you are unable to do some of your household chores, you may claim at settlement or court the assistance you received (even if you didn't pay for it), but it should be documented. See Chapter 5.

9. You fail to obtain a Work Capacity Evaluation that simulates the demands of your job.
A Work Capacity Evaluation can prove your limitations regarding your ability to work and perform household chores.

At some point, ICBC will insist that you are able to work full time, or your finances may force you to return to work. In these situations, this assessment can be invaluable. A lawyer will arrange and pay for a Work Capacity Evaluation. See Chapter 19.

10. You do not keep a regular pain diary.
If you don't recover quickly from your injury, an ICBC lawyer may eventually ask you questions about your pain over time. If you haven't kept a regular pain diary, this information will be very difficult for you to provide. See Chapter 7.

11. You were unable to identify the driver of the vehicle that caused your accident.
ICBC has very strict requirements for identifying the driver who caused your accident. If these requirements aren't met, it is likely that your entire claim will be destroyed. See Chapter 8.

12. If a friend or relative caused the accident, you do not want to claim for your injuries.
You may be concerned that your friend or relative will lose their safe driving discount if you claim for your injuries. ICBC will reduce the discount anyway, based on the repair cost to the other vehicle. In reality, your claim for damages is with ICBC, under your friend or relative's insurance.

CHAPTER 2

YOUR FIRST MEETING WITH ICBC'S ADJUSTER

Here are some answers to questions you might have.

Q: ICBC scheduled me to go to a claim centre tomorrow to make a claim. Do I have to attend right away? I was injured only 3 days ago.
A: This depends upon whether you are:
- a driver who was very clearly not at fault or a passenger, cyclist or pedestrian, versus
- a driver who may have been at fault in the accident, and the owner of that vehicle.

If you are a driver who was very clearly not at fault, a passenger, cyclist, or pedestrian, don't let ICBC pressure you to go in right away. You can cancel the appointment and reschedule it in a few weeks when you are ready. Your obligation to see ICBC is governed by this regulation:

"Where an accident occurs for which benefits are provided under this Part, the insured shall
- **promptly** give the corporation **notice** of the accident [ICBC Dial-a-Claim: 604-520-8222],
- **not later than 30 days** from the date of the accident, **mail** to the corporation by registered mail, or deliver to the nearest claims centre of the corporation, **a written report** on the accident with particulars of the circumstances in which the accident occurred and the consequences of the accident [NOTE that it **does not require you to be interviewed** by an adjuster or to sign the statement he or she prepares], and
- within 90 days from the date of the accident **furnish** the corporation with a **proof of claim** in a form authorized by the corporation [this is a standard ICBC one page insurance claim form].

ICBC is not liable to an insured who, to the prejudice of the corporation, fails to comply with this section."

This means that before you meet with an ICBC adjuster, you have time to:
- overcome your initial shock, stress and acute pain,
- prepare for the interview, and
- meet with a lawyer if you wish.

If you are a driver or vehicle owner and there is a possibility that you or the driver of your vehicle were at fault in the accident, then you may be able to put off your appointment for a few days to obtain legal advice. Don't delay any longer than this, as you will want ICBC to cover any damage claims against you. Your obligation to see

ICBC soon after the accident is very strict. It is governed by the following regulation under your "third party liability" insurance coverage:

73 (1) An insured shall

- **promptly** give the corporation **written notice, with all available particulars**, of
  o any accident involving death, injury, damage or loss in which he or a vehicle owned or operated by him has been involved,
  o any claim made in respect of the accident.
- **co-operate** with the corporation in the investigation... or defence of a claim or action,
- **allow the corporation to inspect an insured vehicle** or its equipment or both **at any reasonable time.**

The corporation is not liable to an insured who, to the prejudice of the corporation, fails to comply with this section.

Q: If I was a passenger or a driver who was clearly not at fault, how should I prepare for my first meeting with ICBC? I was injured.

A: An ICBC adjuster will interview you and prepare a statement for you to sign. This is a very important document. ICBC often uses claimants' statements against them at a later date. One reason ICBC might use your statement later is to demonstrate that you are not believable (because your statement is not completely truthful), so be prepared to give a completely accurate statement. This is not the easiest thing to do since our memories are imperfect.

This is a key question in your injury claim: "What difference did the injury make in your life?" The adjuster will ask you for details about your health, work history, hobbies and sports before the accident.

Your pre-accident health

Most people find it difficult to clearly remember details of their health prior to an accident. For example, how many times did you see your chiropractor, physiotherapist or family doctor due to neck or back pain in the two years before the accident? If you had related health concerns before your accident, phone the receptionist of your chiropractor, physiotherapist or other treatment practitioner to find out the dates and number of times you received treatment. You may also be able to get a computer printout of this. Visit your family doctor and bring a notepad. Ask him or her to quickly review with you the clinical notes about your related complaints and the appointment dates when you made the complaints.

Your pre-accident income

Your income tax returns and T4's are important documents in proving your earnings history and your loss of income. When you visit an ICBC adjuster, bring photocopies of your tax returns for the two years before the accident. Also bring a copy of your most recent pay stub for the current year - if you have worked the entire year and it shows your year-to-date income. Otherwise, bring copies of each pay stub for the current year. This will enable ICBC to more quickly assist you with your financial loss.

Your hobbies and sports
Think about what non-work activities have occupied most of your free time over the past year or two, and make a list in order of importance. Your believability could be placed in doubt if, for example, your statement indicates you cannot ski anymore and you neglected to mention that you had skied only once in the previous 3 years.

Your injuries
If you did not mention in your statement a part of your body where you experienced pain or discomfort and it later becomes a long-term problem, you may have difficulty proving that the accident caused this problem. ICBC's standard argument is that people often experience pain when they have not been in a car accident. Your doctor may neglect to note in his records a certain complaint within the first month or so following the accident, even though you told him or her about it. Doctors often do not write down every complaint.

List your injuries from most severe to least severe and from head to toe so as to not miss anything, and take your list with you to the meeting with the adjuster. Be sure to note if you have dizziness or imbalance. List any psychological problems you are having such as memory, concentration and reading problems, anxiety, fear of driving, irritability, sleeplessness, nightmares, flashbacks or intrusive thoughts of the accident. Do not go into great detail, but think about the severity and pattern of each area of pain such as your neck, low back and left leg. Is your neck pain, for example, mild, mild to moderate, moderate, moderate to severe or severe? For roughly what portion of your waking hours is it at each level of severity?

Your seatbelt and headrest
The adjuster will likely ask if you were wearing your seatbelt and how high your headrest was adjusted in relation to the back of your head. The purpose of these questions is for ICBC to determine whether it will be able to reduce your damage claim by a certain percentage due to your failing to take reasonable care.

The accident itself
In most accidents, one or more drivers will be found liable for your injuries. If ICBC is the insurer for both drivers, then it doesn't really matter how much responsibility is applied to each driver if you were a passenger. As a passenger, however, you should be prepared to answer questions about the accident, including those relating to time and distance.

If you wish to further prepare for answering questions about the accident itself, please see the answer to the next question below.

Q: How should I prepare for my first meeting with ICBC? (For drivers, cyclists and pedestrians possibly at fault)
A: If, for example, you are found 40% to blame for an accident, you will only be able to recover 60% of the assessed value of your damages; therefore, it is extremely important for you to be very well prepared before an adjuster interviews you.

Some of the questions the adjuster may ask you are:
* Did you have time to brake?
* What was your speed before you applied your brakes and at impact?
* How far away from the other vehicle or the intersection were you when you first saw the other vehicle or when you first saw it turning?
* How many seconds before impact was this?

These are very difficult questions to answer, especially if you haven't had time to think carefully about them and the adjuster is expecting your instant answer so he or she can type it out. It would be very useful for you to return to the accident scene before you visit the ICBC adjuster so you can reconstruct the accident in your own mind. This may be a traumatic experience for you, but it will be well worth it. You will want to:
* check for skid marks and debris from each vehicle and photograph them,
* measure distances on the basis of meters or number of car lengths,
* count out the seconds before impact, and
* check your speedometer while traveling at the speed you recall going just before you braked and just before the accident.

Do not discuss the accident with witnesses or anyone else involved in it. If you do, the credibility of both you and the other person will be reduced. It would mean that you are no longer relying on your own memory - your memory would then be contaminated by the recollections of others. At least one of you will eventually admit that these discussions occurred.

It is best to have a friend, relative, lawyer or private investigator speak to witnesses and other people involved in the accident.

In order to prepare for questions on subjects other than the accident itself, please see the answers to the two questions above.

Q: What if no driver is at fault?
A: ICBC or the court might conclude that no driver was at fault in your accident. If this happens, you will not be able to recover any damages, even though you were an innocent passenger in the accident. Examples of such accidents are:
* when a vehicle collides with an animal on the road,
* when a vehicle hits black ice or an isolated patch of snow or other slippery substance on the road which could not have reasonably been anticipated, or
* when a vehicle's tire blows, even though the tire was apparently in good condition.

Your driver may be found at fault in these circumstances:
* if he or she was driving too fast for road conditions, or
* if he or she was not fully paying attention to the road ahead.

Under these circumstances, you may want to obtain legal advice before you visit ICBC.

Think carefully about whether any of the circumstances placing someone at fault apply to your case before you visit ICBC's adjuster.

Q: After the adjuster prepares the statement, should I sign it?
A: In most cases, it is best to tell the adjuster that you will take the statement home to read it and will sign after you've determined if it is entirely accurate. You may change the statement any way you want to make it entirely accurate. Initial any changes before you sign it. If the adjuster's statement is very inaccurate or incomplete, you may prepare an amended version of your statement and then sign and date this version. The problem with changing your statement after you leave the ICBC claim centre, however, is that the adjuster could later testify that he is certain he wrote down exactly what you told him or her. This is why it is so important that you prepare yourself well before the adjuster interviews you.

It may be safe for you to sign your statement at the claim centre after the adjuster prepares it if:
- you were in excellent health prior to the accident,
- you did not have any previous problems similar to your injuries,
- your claim for income loss is simple and straight forward and
- there is no possibility that you could be at fault.

CHAPTER 3

HOW ICBC SHOULD HELP YOU NOW WITH TREATMENT

Q: Will ICBC cover the cost of physiotherapy, chiropractic, massage therapy or dental treatments?
A: Your insurance policy with ICBC states that ICBC shall "pay as benefits all reasonable expenses incurred by the insured as a result of the injury for necessary medical, surgical, dental, hospital, ambulance or professional nursing services, or for necessary physical therapy, chiropractic treatment, occupational therapy or speech therapy or for prosthesis or orthosis."

This, however, is subject to a few conditions:
• If you have an extended health policy that covers such treatments, ICBC does not have to pay for any treatments until you have exhausted your coverage under this policy. This can be unfavourable if you plan to use your annual allowance for treatment under your extended health policy for another medical condition. Fortunately, adjusters frequently don't enforce this condition.
• ICBC will rarely agree to pay for more than one type of treatment at a time.
• ICBC has to pre-approve a certain number of treatments.
• You will need a medical or dental recommendation for the specific treatment. While this usually comes from your family doctor in a medical report form completed early in your claim, a note from your doctor may suffice.
• ICBC will only pay fees in the amount set out in its regulations, even though most physiotherapists, chiropractors and massage therapists charge more. As a result, you may have to make up the difference - up to $40 for the first appointment, and $10 to $20 for each subsequent appointment. This can be very onerous for injured people who are not employed. Some practitioners do base their fees close to ICBC's prescribed schedule, however, so phone around to compare fees. You may not have to pay a large user fee.

ICBC will often reimburse your user fees on a monthly basis if you did not cause the collision. Ask your adjuster if ICBC is willing to do this for you. If so, the reimbursement will be considered an advance on your final settlement or court award.

Q: How do I obtain funding for treatment by a psychologist for my pain, stress and depression?
A: The Medical Services Plan of B.C. covers treatment by a psychiatrist if a family doctor refers a patient. It does not cover psychological treatments.

Psychologists cannot prescribe drugs. Their techniques such as cognitive behavioural therapy have been shown to complement the medications prescribed by physicians. Some psychologists specialize in treatment after trauma; others specialize in pain management techniques.

Check your extended health plan. Many of them cover some psychological treatments each calendar year. Some employers have "employee assistance" plans that will fund treatment by a psychologist.

With a recommendation from a family doctor, ICBC should pay for up to four sessions with a psychologist (if no extended health plan will cover this). ICBC may also fund additional sessions based on the treating psychologist's recommendations.

Ask your family doctor if he or she can recommend a psychologist. You - not your family doctor - will have to arrange the initial appointment. Lawyers who do a lot of ICBC injury work may know the track records of some psychologists.

CHAPTER 4

HOW ICBC SHOULD HELP YOU NOW
WITH DISABILITY BENEFITS

Q. What is the maximum I am entitled to receive in disability benefits from ICBC?
A: If you meet the restrictive conditions of ICBC's Accident Benefits policy, you are entitled to a maximum of only $1,300 per month unless you purchased extended coverage before your collision. You are entitled to less than $1,300 per month if your gross income averaged less than $1,733 per month during the 12 months before the collision. In this case, you would be entitled to only 75% of your average gross earnings during the 12 months before the collision. This amount is very low - the only saving grace is that you do not have to pay income tax on these disability benefits.

Q: What conditions must I meet to be entitled to immediate disability benefits from ICBC?
A: There is a one-week waiting period. You must then meet several pre-conditions set out in your ICBC insurance policy:
- You must be either an employed or self-employed person.
- If you are unemployed, you must have been employed for six months during the year before the collision.
- You must be "totally disabled... from engaging in employment or an occupation for which you are reasonably suited by education, training or experience."
- You must be totally disabled within 20 days after the collision.
- You must have been the occupant of a vehicle licensed in B.C. when you were injured, or
- You must be a cyclist or pedestrian who was struck by a vehicle named in an ICBC insurance policy, or
- You must be a member of the household of someone named in an ICBC insurance policy.

Q: I am entitled to disability benefits under a disability plan I have through work and also under a policy I purchased myself. Am I also entitled to receive ICBC wage replacement?
A: You are entitled from ICBC a top-up of the difference between 75% of your average pre-accident wage and, if less, the amount you are entitled to from all other disability insurance policies purchased by you or by a group such as your union or your employer. This is to a maximum from ICBC of $1,300 per month.

If you are not entitled to ICBC disability benefits, you or your lawyer should try to persuade your adjuster to pay you advances on your final claim for damages against the other driver (who would be insured by ICBC under his third party liability insurance.) This money is more beneficial to you now than it would be in the future when you are back at work and you resolve your damages claim.

Q: I am entitled to sickness benefits under my Employment Insurance. Am I also entitled to receive ICBC wage replacement?
A: Your ICBC policy does not allow you to receive ICBC disability benefits during the period that you are entitled to receive Employment Insurance (EI) sickness benefits. This applies even if you choose to not apply for EI. An exception to this rule is if you are entitled to more under your ICBC wage replacement policy than you are from EI. In this case, ICBC must top up your EI to what you would be entitled to receive from ICBC.

While you are waiting to receive your EI sickness benefits you or your lawyer should try to persuade your adjuster to pay you advances on your final claim for damages.

Q: Do I have any recourse if my employer's disability insurer cuts off my benefits? Do the same rules apply if ICBC cuts off my disability or rehabilitation benefits?
A: You may have recourse. For years our courts were very easy on punishing disability insurers that improperly cut off benefits. The courts have finally become somewhat tougher on them. As a result, insurers are now somewhat more nervous about terminating disability benefits.

ICBC is your own insurer for ICBC disability, homemaker and rehabilitation benefits. The following principles apply equally to ICBC and to your disability insurer:

* You may have claims for aggravated and punitive damages in addition to a claim for the reinstatement of your benefits.
* Aggravated damages are available if an insured establishes that a breach of a contract by an insurer caused him or her mental distress.

The B.C. Court of Appeal wrote the following in support of its award of $100,000 in punitive damages in a 2004 decision called *Fidler v. Sun Life Assurance Co. of Canada:*

"Having concluded that Sun Life breached the duty of utmost good faith it owed to Ms. Fidler, I am persuaded that its breach is such a marked departure from ordinary standards of decent behaviour as to be deserving of punishment in the form of **punitive damages**...

In my view, punitive damages are required in this case to denounce Sun Life's conduct and to deter it and other insurers from engaging in this type of conduct in the future.

... the aggravated damages of $20,000 awarded in this case are insufficient to mark the court's disapprobation of Sun Life's conduct. The insurer's refusal to pay benefits to a vulnerable insured for over five years resulted in more than $50,000 in benefits (and pre-judgment interest) having been withheld. In my view, a rationally proportionate penalty in these circumstances is the sum of $100,000. I would award punitive damages in that amount."

CHAPTER 5

HOW ICBC SHOULD HELP YOU NOW AND LATER
WITH HOUSEHOLD CHORES

Q: I need to hire someone to help clean my house. Am I entitled to financial help from ICBC <u>right away</u>?
A: ICBC may be required to pay you up to $145 per week to cover your expenses of hiring a person to do your household chores. This is under your ICBC Accident Benefits, "Part 7" of your insurance with ICBC.

In order to be entitled to these benefits you must establish that you are "substantially and continuously" disabled from regularly performing **most** of your household tasks. Your doctor may be willing to back you up with a note to this effect and to provide an estimate of the number of hours per week of assistance you need. If so, obtain a note from him or her stating this. Give the note to your adjuster and ask him or her to reimburse you or pay directly these expenses under your Accident Benefits.

If ICBC agrees that you are entitled to these benefits it will likely insist on hiring someone to attend your home. This person will likely have to regularly complete a form about what she observes at your home. This is a major invasion of your privacy. You should insist on hiring someone yourself and having ICBC reimburse you. Obtain a few written quotes to show ICBC that you obtained a reasonable price for the help you need.
If ICBC refuses to reimburse you for these expenses you can claim them as part of your final settlement or court award. You will need detailed invoices plus supporting evidence from a medical person.

ICBC does not have to reimburse you under your Accident Benefits if you pay a family member to do certain chores.

Q: I am not able to do all the household chores that I did before the collision. I was unable to pay someone to help me. So my husband and children are doing a lot of what I used to do. Are they entitled to be compensated for this?
A: You are entitled to compensation at the end for your loss of homemaking capacity. Your family members do not make this claim. The law considers this your loss so you make the claim.

It is no longer necessary in law to establish that you paid someone to do what you were not able to do. However you must prove how much time other people spent doing chores that you did before the collision. Each family member and friend who helps you should write down every week the chores that he or she did for you and how much time he or she spent doing each chore.

This claim applies equally to indoor and outdoor work and to chores that either a man or a woman can no longer do.

Your claim will be much stronger if you have evidence from a medical person as to the number of hours of assistance you needed over time. Speak to your physician about this every few months. Some physicians will put in their notes their opinion as to the number of hours of assistance you need. This will be of little or no value unless your physician bases his or her opinion on a physical examination. Some physicians will not be very keen on doing this.

There is another profession whose members provide such opinions for legal purposes on a regular basis. They are "certified work capacity evaluators" who are usually occupational therapists. They will spend several hours testing your physical abilities. (See chapter 19)

Q: Am I entitled to claim for the cost of assistance I will need in the future with my household chores?
A: Yes, you are. However you will need a solid medical report on what chores you are unable to do now and how many hours per week it would take an experienced person to do these chores for you. A certified work capacity evaluator is usually the best person to provide such a report. You will **also** need a report from a medical specialist containing the clearest prognosis possible. This is a prediction of your future ability to function over the short medium and long term.

CHAPTER 6

YOUR MEDICAL RECORDS - THE EXTENT OF YOUR RIGHT TO PRIVACY

Q: Which of my medical records is ICBC entitled to see?

A: ICBC will try to obtain as many of your medical records as possible from before and after your accident. The courts do not allow ICBC to go on a "fishing expedition" through your pre-accident records. ICBC must establish that there is something relevant to your injury claim in these records.

You have the right to privacy regarding medical records that may be embarrassing and confidential, but only if they are not relevant to your claim for damages. The definition of relevancy in our legal system is very broad and includes documents that contain information which may directly or indirectly enable ICBC to advance its own case or damage your case.

Advise your lawyer if you think there are some notations in one or more of your doctors' files that are embarrassing and irrelevant to your claim. He or she may then obtain the records. You can review them and tell your lawyer exactly which notations or documents you do not want disclosed. Your lawyer will then advise you whether you are entitled to not disclose these records to ICBC.

Q: What is the wording of the medical consent that ICBC wants me to sign?

A: The wording of ICBC's standard authorization is exceedingly broad. It states:
"I, **authorize** every medical practitioner ...**to provide** any representative of the Insurance Corporation of British Columbia ... any and all **records**, x-rays, information and evidence in their possession ...including **medical history and physical condition both prio**r and subsequent to the above date, <u>**regardless of lapsed time,**</u> providing the information **relates, in some way**, to any injuries sustained on or about the above date."

Note that the form gives no direction as to what type of pre-accident records do not relate in some way to your injuries. It also allows for very many years of pre-accident records to be released. Ask yourself whether it is likely your doctor will sift through your files and pull out materials that don't relate in some way to your injuries.

Q: Do I have to sign the medical consent form the adjuster wants me to sign?

A: No, ICBC accident benefit regulations do not require you to sign it. If you do not have a lawyer, however, ICBC will likely not provide you with benefits unless you sign the form as it stands or with reasonable amendments to it. **Examples of reasonable amendments** are that you could prohibit access to your pre-accident medical records earlier than six months before your accident and to the records of your gynaecologist and to the records in your family physician's file respecting gynaecological and psychiatric issues. These records are likely irrelevant to your claim and it would be embarrassing to you if they were disclosed to ICBC adjusters and managers.

Q: How can I revoke the ICBC medical consent I signed or at least ensure that my doctor does not release irrelevant or old records prior to my accident?
A: Many physicians will release your medical records that were created before your accident when they receive your completed consent form from ICBC - even if the records have little or nothing to do with your injuries and are personal and embarrassing. Lawyers for injured people almost always revoke this consent when they advise ICBC that they are involved.

If you signed ICBC's prescribed consent without changing it, you may want to write a letter to each of the physicians who treated you before the accident. It might read something like this:
"[Date]
Dr. [name]
Re: [Your name]; instructions to not release medical records to ICBC created prior to [date of motor vehicle accident] MVA
Please keep this letter on the inside front or top of my file at all times. I was injured in a motor vehicle accident on [date]. ICBC asked me to sign a very broad medical authorization. I signed it because I did not want to harm my chances of receiving ICBC's assistance. I did not intend it to include the release of any of my clinical records prior to my accident. If you feel that you must send ICBC any of my pre-accident clinical records, please do not do so until we have reviewed these records together face-to-face. I want to ensure that no irrelevant clinical records are released to ICBC. I also want us to decide together how much time before the accident, if at all, relevant records should be released. Thank you for respecting my privacy.
Yours Truly"

Deliver this letter personally to your physician. If you disagree with what your physician wants to disclose to ICBC, you could prepare and personally deliver to ICBC and your doctor a letter as follows:
"To: ICBC
And to: Dr. [name]
I hereby revoke the authorization I signed giving ICBC authority to obtain any of my medical records.
Yours Truly,
[your name]"

CHAPTER 7

KEEPING A PAIN DIARY

Q: Is it valuable to keep a diary?

A: If you have significant injuries that do not heal within a year or so, you may end up suing the person who caused the accident. At a meeting called an "examination for discovery" - which may take place a year or two after your accident - ICBC's lawyer will ask you questions under oath, about:

a) your health prior to the accident,

b) your level of pain and limitations over time since the accident,

c) what rehabilitation efforts you made over time.

Injured people generally have difficulty remembering how they felt a year or two before; the human mind seems to blot this out to some extent. Medication also tends to blur one's memory. It would be very helpful, therefore, to be able refresh your memory by referring to a diary.

Unfortunately, a diary may not be confidential.

You will likely not be allowed to refer to your diary when ICBC's lawyer asks you questions. If you have to provide ICBC's lawyer with your diary, however, he may use it to later point out contradictions between what you said under oath and what you wrote in your diary. Contradictions are one of the surest ways to harm a person's credibility.

Q: How extensive should my diary be?

A: Brevity is usually best in a diary. There are a few reasons for this:

- During your recovery period, you will likely want to spend as little time as possible focusing on your pain and disability;
- You will eventually need to read your diary in preparation for answering questions under oath. If your diary is too extensive, you will likely have difficulty remembering what you wrote;
- If you have a large diary, it will take you many hours to read and summarize the essence of your diary regarding your condition during each month or season. No one in the legal system is interested in a daily or weekly account of your problems.

You may find it best to sit down at the same time every week or second week and spend 10 minutes or so summarizing the past week or two. In this summary, you could describe five things:

- your pattern and degree of pain,
- your sleep interference,
- whom you saw for treatment and when,
- the activities you tried and the result, and
- the amount of time you spent doing active rehabilitation.

The following words are very useful when describing your pattern and degree of pain:
• mild pain (mi) ; mild to moderate pain (mi-mo); moderate pain (mo); moderate to severe pain (mo-sev); severe pain (sev) and very severe (v-sev) pain

Some people prefer using numbers to describe their pain - 10 being the worst pain imaginable, 0 being no pain and 4 to 6 being the mid-point between the two extremes.

Many people have better and worse days. You could write, for example, that you had three better and four worse days during the week, and then describe your pain pattern on an average better day and worse day, i.e., "on a better day - sev pain - about 10%, mo to sev - 20%; mo - 40%; mi to mo - 20%; mi - 10%." Of course, these would only be your best estimates. No one can be mathematically precise about this.

You could describe your sleep loss by stating:
• the approximate number of hours and fractions of hours it takes you to get to sleep on better and worse days,
• about how often you wake up, and
• about how long you think you are awake per night after first getting to sleep.

For example, on better days,
• 1.5 hours to get to sleep,
• wake up about 3 to 5 times, and
• awake about 2 hours during the night.

You can use shorthand to record this information.

You could describe in a simple table your exercise program by stating the approximate number of hours or minutes you devote each day to each of stretching, strengthening and cardiovascular activity. This information is important to counter the standard ICBC argument that you did not do enough exercise over time and, therefore, your slow recovery is your own fault.

You could describe activities you tried and had trouble with, or activities that later increased your pain.

If you're on a graduated return-to-work program, note the number of hours you worked each day.

Q: How do I keep my diary confidential?
A: Communication between a client and his or her lawyer is "privileged." This means that a judge will not force you or your lawyer to disclose the privileged document. If, instead of keeping a diary, you write your lawyer a letter or a series or letters about your ongoing condition, the court might consider this correspondence privileged (although there is no guarantee). If you know which lawyer you intend to use at some point, you could write that lawyer a letter about your ongoing condition. It would also help if you spoke with the lawyer about your case before you started your diary.

Eventually, a question will arise as to whether the ongoing letter was intended to be a letter to your lawyer or just a diary notation for yourself, which is certainly not privileged. It would be valuable, therefore, for you to use an inexpensive scribbler or other bound document to write your lawyer or intended lawyer, and to write on the first page of the scribbler a dated, formal letter to the lawyer. The following is an example:

Your name

Your address

Date

Lawyer's name, firm and address

Dear Sir [or Madam]

Re: my MVA of [date] & my progress

The following is a summary of my condition over time and my rehab efforts. I hope you find it of value.

I would be pleased to discuss it with you once you have had a chance to read it.

Yours Truly,

[your name]

It is best to use your own words in your letter to your lawyer or intended lawyer.

CHAPTER 8

HIT & RUN CLAIMS: THEY NEED TO BE DONE RIGHT

Q: After my vehicle accident, the other driver left the scene before I could obtain his licence plate number. Do I have a claim for damages? What do I do?
A: You should obtain legal advice immediately in the case of a hit and run accident. You may have a claim for damages against ICBC under your own insurance policy or the policy of a member of your household, but you must strictly comply with the conditions of your insurance policy. These conditions were created in an effort to avoid fraudulent hit and run claims.

You must make "all reasonable efforts" to ascertain the identity of the unknown driver and owner. A judge or jury is ultimately responsible for deciding whether or not you made "all reasonable efforts" if ICBC denies that you did so. Case law has developed as to what this phrase means. Below are some of the steps you could take to help ensure you meet the requirements:

* Contact the **police** immediately (this is mandatory);
* Look for **debris and skid marks** from the vehicles at the accident scene. Measure the skid marks and take photographs that clearly show the location of this evidence. Collect the debris (if the police do not do this) or first ask a lawyer whether you should have an accident reconstruction engineer attend the scene right away;
* Phone ICBC **Dial-a-Claim**. You can't report hit and run claims on-line;
* **Speak to residents and businesses** located near the accident scene. Did anyone see the accident or its aftermath? If so, did they note the colour, model or plate number of the other vehicle? Did they note the names of any witnesses?
* Near the scene, put up large, clearly-written **signs seeking witnesses** to the accident. Take photographs of the signs. Use the date stamp option on the camera to show when the photographs were taken;
* Put **ads in newspapers** seeking witnesses to the accident. Tear out the entire page from the newspaper to prove what dates you ran the ads;
* **Follow up with the police officer** responsible for investigating the accident a few times by phone to see if he or she has obtained any leads. Remember, the person who hit you and left the scene will likely need to have his vehicle repaired;
* **make detailed notes** of every step you take to ascertain the identities of the other driver and owner of the vehicle.

CHAPTER 9

IF YOU WERE WORKING AT THE TIME THE COLLISION OCCURRED - WORKSAFEBC

Q: I was working at the time of my collision. ICBC claims that the driver who was at fault was also working at the time and that I therefore have no claim against ICBC. Is ICBC right?
A: If the other driver was not a "worker" as defined by the Workers Compensation Act, you have may have to decide whether to make a WorkSafeBC claim or to claim damages against ICBC; however, ICBC may refuse to pay you disability benefits or fund your rehabilitation on the basis that you were a "worker." (See the other questions in this section on this issue.)

If both you and the other driver are found to be "workers," then you are not entitled to claim damages against ICBC. Your claim is against WorkSafeBC.

The Workers' Compensation Appeal Tribunal (WCAT) has exclusive jurisdiction to decide whether a person was, at the time of a motor vehicle collision, a worker and covered by WorkSafeBC. Our courts have no power to decide this issue.

You should definitely obtain legal advice as to the likelihood of the tribunal finding the other driver to be a "worker" at the time of the collision.

Q: I was working at the time of the. The other driver was not working. Am I entitled to receive ICBC rehabilitation and disability benefits and to claim damages from ICBC if I decide not to make a WorkSafeBC claim?
A: Your ICBC Accident Benefits policy gives ICBC a virtual "out" of paying you rehabilitation or disability benefits if you decide not to make a WorkSafeBC claim. If you do not make a WorkSafeBC claim, you have the right to make a claim for damages.

You may have a generous extended health plan and good short and long term disability plans through your employer, or you may be entitled to Employment Insurance sickness benefits. If so, you may be able to manage without ICBC's assistance until you finally resolve your claim for damages.

Some injured people feel financially pressured to make a WorkSafeBC claim, even though they do not want to deal with WorkSafeBC. Be sure to speak to a lawyer before accepting any money or funding of treatment from WorkSafeBC. You can then decide if it is in your best interests to continue with your WorkSafeBC claim or to pursue a claim for damages against ICBC.

If you elect to pursue a WorkSafeBC claim and the other driver was not a "worker" at the time of the collision, WorkSafeBC's legal department may "stand in your shoes" to pursue a claim for damages against ICBC to recover what it paid you, and more. When

WorkSafeBC resolves this claim, you may receive some money - after WorkSafeBC pays itself first. In this case, WorkSafeBC would have all the decision-making power in its claim against ICBC and you would have no right to reject an offer from ICBC that WorkSafeBC BC wants to accept. WorkSafeBC would decide how much to pay itself from the award, taking into consideration monies it may pay you for future compensation.

It is, therefore, in your best interests to obtain legal advice before electing to pursue a WorkSafeBC claim.

CHAPTER 10

ICBC SURVEILLANCE

Q: I get the feeling that someone is watching me. Am I correct?
A: You may be correct. This is one of the main tools that ICBC uses to defend claims for damages. Sometimes an ICBC investigator will sit in a parked van on the street where an injured person lives. He will often then follow the person and video his or her activities.

Q: Is it legal for ICBC's investigators to videotape injured people?
A: Yes, as long as the investigator does not unreasonably invade a person's privacy. For example, if the investigator is on the street videotaping you in your garden, this is likely legal. If he is outside videotaping you (through your window) in your living room, this is likely illegal.

Q: How does ICBC use the videotaped evidence obtained by its investigators to defend injury claims?
A: ICBC is required to disclose the video evidence it obtains just 7 days before the date of your trial.

If you start a lawsuit, eventually an ICBC lawyer will ask you questions under oath at an "examination for discovery." The lawyer will ask you what you were unable to do during various periods since your accident. If your sworn testimony or what you tell various doctors (including the doctor ICBC hires) contradicts what the video shows you doing, it could be very harmful to your claim. If the videotape ICBC obtains is consistent with your injuries and what you claim are your limitations, ICBC will likely never disclose that it has video evidence. The evidence on the videotape, however, may cause ICBC to offer you a larger settlement than it might have otherwise offered.

During your mediation, ICBC may show you extracts of video it thinks will harm your case. This is part of its negotiation strategy. You should insist on seeing the entire videotape - not just snippets of it. You may have done a specific activity in an effort to live a normal life and then paid the price a few minutes or hours later.

Q: Do judges find video evidence valuable in helping them reach their decisions in injury cases?
A: Sometimes a judge will find the video evidence very helpful. The following is an extract of a judge's decision in the case of *Friesen versus Hsu*:

> "Despite the plaintiff's assertion she is totally disabled from any employment, even part-time, a surveillance video... shows the plaintiff walking and moving about fluidly and freely. She is seen getting into the passenger side of a van and a car, seemingly without difficulty. She is seen to pull the car door shut while seated in the car, seemingly without difficulty. She is seen carrying a large but apparently empty cooler, as well as bags and garbage."

Other times, a judge will find that the video evidence is a waste of the court's time. If, for example, the investigator's bills to ICBC show that he spent 60 hours observing you, but only five minutes of his video show that you were performing strenuous activity, the value of the video is minimal.

A video rarely shows how the injured person appears a few hours after attempting an activity.

If a settlement cannot be reached, some injury claims are decided by a jury. A jury may be so upset by ICBC interfering with the injured person's privacy that it may make a larger award for damages than it would have otherwise made.

Q: Does ICBC ever combine video surveillance with an ICBC medical examination?
A: Yes. ICBC has been known to hire a private investigator to videotape injured people from when they leave their home to attend an ICBC medical examination until they arrive back home after the examination. ICBC is hoping to show that the injured person's behaviour during the medical examination is different from what it was before or after the examination.

In addition, if the doctor ICBC hires is aware that ICBC has a video showing you doing certain activities, he may ask you about all the activities you claim you cannot do.

Q: How do I defend myself against surveillance?
A: Discuss with your doctor whether it is advisable for you to live as normal a life as possible and to try to do as much activity as possible, even though you may suffer afterwards for doing it. You would then be following medical advice when you do certain activities.

If there is a vehicle parked on your street with a person in it, phone the local police detachment and ask them to check out this unusual activity. For all you know, the person could be a burglar "casing" your house.

Consider being assessed periodically by a certified work capacity evaluator. He or she will spend between four hours and two days testing your abilities and determining what you can and cannot do on a sustained basis. See Chapter 19.

Note in your diary the more strenuous activities you attempt and the consequences you suffer after doing them (e.g., carrying groceries to and from your car, picking up or playing with a child, etc.). It's easy to forget what you did and what you later paid for in the way of pain.

ICBC is unlikely to admit to having a video of you if it does not help them. One way of determining if it has a video of you is to make a Freedom of Information request. This sometimes discloses an adjuster's notes of decisions on whether or not to order video surveillance.

Q: How should I prepare for my examination for discovery regarding possible video surveillance of me?
A: When ICBC's lawyer asks you questions under oath at your examination for discovery, you should clearly admit to attempting various activities but explain the consequences of doing the activities.

If ICBC's lawyer asks you questions to see if you could do certain activities at a certain time, it may mean that ICBC has some videotaped evidence during that period. Many lawyers are more subtle in their questioning, so you should prepare for your examination for discovery by reviewing your diary to see what activities you attempted but suffered pain afterwards.

Q: Can I turn the tables and use the video evidence ICBC obtains to strengthen my case?
A: You may be able to use the videos ICBC obtains to strengthen your own case - assuming that you didn't deny doing the activities that the video records. For example, friends and family members may explain that even though you knew you would pay dearly every week and would have to rest for a few days afterwards due to pain, you deemed it so important to do certain activities with your children that you did them anyway.

Q: Will judges punish ICBC if the investigator turns his video camera on and off so that the video does not accurately show the whole story?
A: The court may punish ICBC for improper video surveillance in a number of ways. The judge might not allow the video to be admitted into evidence. If a trial is before a jury, and members of the jury are outraged by the conduct of the investigator, the jury may be motivated to make a larger award for damages than it may have done otherwise. The judge may also award the injured person "special costs" if he or she concludes that ICBC knowingly used misleading video evidence. This means that ICBC must reimburse the injured person a much greater than normal portion of his or her legal fees.

CHAPTER 11

VALUING DAMAGES: PAIN AND SUFFERING

Our courts are required to break down an injured person's damages award into various categories or "heads" of damages, so when we negotiate with ICBC we break down our clients' offers and counter-offers into various heads of damages.

Q: How do the courts and ICBC decide how much to award an injured person for pain and suffering?
A: The amount that a court awards an injured person for pain and suffering depends upon whether the case is being decided by a judge or by a jury. When ICBC is pushed to the wall and a trial date is fast approaching, the amount it decides to offer is based on several factors, including what it thinks is the likely range that a judge or jury will award the injured person if the case goes to trial.

Judges try to maintain consistency amongst awards for a similar injury and consequences of the injury. In order to do this, they review a number of written decisions of other trial judges and the Court of Appeal. They are not bound by what other judges have awarded in similar cases, but those awards give them guidance as to the range. Some judges tend to make awards at the higher end of the range; others lean more towards the lower end of the range.

If either side in a lawsuit chooses a jury to decide how much to award an injured person, the law does not allow the judge or the lawyers to advise the jury what range judges have awarded for pain and suffering in such cases - except in "severe" cases. In these cases, the judge informs the jury that the law in Canada has placed a cap of about $320,000 on awards for pain and suffering. Most members of the public are shocked by how low this cap has been set for a person who is catastrophically injured. Fortunately, a jury may also award damages for other categories of damages. This can make the total damage award very large in spite of the cap on pain and suffering awards.

Juries tend to be generous if they:
• admire the injured person's struggle to overcome his or her injuries,
• believe the injuries have had a profound impact on the injured person's life, and either see significant damages to vehicles or hear an engineer to explain that the collision forces on the injured person were great.
• are presented with evidence that allows them to see the damage to the injured person and not just take his word for it. Examples of this would be: MRI's, x-rays, medical diagrams, medical models, objective physical test results, scars and limps.

Q: Who gets to decide whether a case will be heard by a judge or by a jury?
A: ICBC (defending the wrongdoer) or the injured person may elect to have a personal injury trial in the Supreme Court of British Columbia decided by either a judge or by a

jury. Certain types of trial procedures for small and medium-sized cases prohibit the use of a jury. One of these procedures may be an appropriate way for you to go.

Whenever a jury trial is permitted, ICBC will usually elect to have cases decided by a jury rather than a judge. It does this by filing a Jury Notice. Closer to the trial date, ICBC may elect to have the trial heard by a judge alone if it feels there is a serious risk that a jury will award an injured person more than a judge would award. Some lawyers for injured people file Jury Notices themselves. If the case does not settle and the injured person's lawyer files the Jury Notice by the required date, ICBC cannot avoid a jury trial if that's what the injured person wants.

If your injuries are serious, talk to a lawyer to find out which of a trial by jury or a judge would be a better strategy in your case.

Q: If I don't settle my claim, how can I get a sense of how much a Supreme Court judge might award me for pain and suffering? Is it possible for me to review court decisions or summaries?

A: You may compare your claim to those of injured people whose cases have been decided by a judge by reading several judges' written reasons explaining their awards. One of the major factors judges consider in making their awards for pain and suffering is how long the injured person has or will in the future suffer significant pain and disability. If you have suffered a serious injury, you will not know your long-term outcome for months or even years, so it is difficult to make a comparison.

If you decide to hire us to handle your claim, we will- -at your request - provide you with ten or fifteen one-page summaries of recent decisions of Supreme Court judges in cases involving injuries similar to yours. We will then meet with you to discuss the case summaries and discuss which ones are more or less severe than the likely consequences of your injuries.

Judges' full decisions are posted on the internet on the judgement database of the "Courts of British Columbia". It goes back to 1996. We print out for clients the full decisions that are most similar to their own situation. Alternatively, we provide clients with the URL's of each of the judges' reasons so that they can read them on the internet.

Most people find it easier to read the full decisions - which can be very long - after they have first read the one-page summaries. There are no summaries on the Court of British Columbia's judgement database. These summaries are created by private services and sold by subscription to lawyers, ICBC and Courthouse libraries.

To get a flavour as to the range of what judges award for pain and suffering for particular injuries of various levels of severity, read a number of the "reasons for judgement" of judges on the database of the "Courts of British Columbia" at: www.courts.gov.bc.ca/

CHAPTER 12

VALUING DAMAGES:
PRE-ACCIDENT PROBLEMS & RETIREES

Q: Before my accident I had arthritis of the neck and experienced occasional flare-ups. My adjuster says I am entitled to less compensation than if I had not had arthritis. Is he correct?

A: Only partially. Physicians generally accept that people with arthritis in the spine experience a more prolonged recovery. ICBC must compensate you for this longer recovery period, but it is not required to compensate you for any pain or limitations you would have had if the accident had not occurred. ICBC is only liable for the additional problems you suffered as a result of the accident. Many people have arthritis but don't have symptoms and don't even know they have it until they are injured and x-rays are taken. A doctor's report summarizing your pre-existing complaints and limitations, your additional problems and how you would have fared had the accident not occurred is very important. Witnesses such as supervisors, friends and family may provide statements and, if necessary, testify as to the changes they have observed in you since the accident.

Q: I am in my 70's. Am I entitled to less compensation for my permanent injury because of my age?

A: A court will take your age into account. If your injury is permanent, for example, you likely would not suffer for as many years as would a younger person with the same type of injury. He has a longer life expectancy. Case law says that any reduction in damages for pain and suffering on account of your age must be done cautiously. Judges accept that in some respects, impairment of an older person can be more serious. As one grows older, one's pleasures and activities may become more limited; therefore, substantial impairment in the amount of activity and movement one can do becomes even more significant.

During negotiations, make it clear to ICBC's adjuster that you are willing to go to court, if necessary. From past experience, adjusters tend to believe that older people are very unlikely to go to court. You should also remind him or her that the judge or jury will apply this case law, which is very supportive of the elderly.

27

CHAPTER 13

VALUING DAMAGES:
COST OF TREATMENT, CARE & ASSISTANCE IN THE FUTURE

Q: What do I have to prove in order to be compensated for expenses I may have in the future due to my injuries for treatment, care and assistance?
A: You are entitled to be compensated for all future expenses that the court concludes are reasonably necessary to promote your mental and physical health in the future. You do not have to go so far as to prove that these expenses are "medically necessary". However you do need medical evidence that the expenses will "promote [your] mental and physical health".

A judge may ask him or her self "what would a reasonably-minded person of ample means be prepared to incur as expenses?" Your entitlement may depend in part on how you lived before the collision. For example, the B.C. Court of Appeal upheld an award of a judge for the cost of altering equipment on the claimant's sailboat so that he could continue to sail in spite of the loss of a finger and dexterity in his hand. The rationale is that sailing would promote his mental and physical health.

Given appropriate evidence, the court may compensate an injured person for the care and domestic work a family member will provide him or her in the future at a reasonable hourly rate. The court may also compensate an injured person on the basis of a trained person providing the services.

You will need solid medical evidence to support a future care claim. Often either nurses or occupational therapists assess injured persons and provide a report as to their future needs and the cost of meeting their needs. In addition, a medical specialist in the field of physical and rehabilitation medicine, a rheumatologist or an orthopaedic surgeon gives an opinion on a person's future needs and how many years into the future these needs will exist.

Usually the injured person's lawyer pays for these assessments and reports and claims reimbursement from ICBC at the end of the case.

CHAPTER 14

VALUING DAMAGES:
COMPENSATION FOR FAMILY MEMBERS OF
THE INJURED PERSON

Q: My husband is doing many of the household chores that I did before my collision. Is he entitled to compensation for this?

A: Our courts look at this as <u>your</u> loss of capacity to perform household chores. Therefore you, rather than your husband, are entitled to compensation for your husband having to do chores that you did before the collision. (See the second Q & A in chapter 5).

Q: My wife took care of me during the first year after my collision when I was unable to fully take care of myself. Is she entitled to compensation for this?

A: You may be entitled to an award "in trust" for her for much of the assistance she provided to you. There are a number of factors that the courts consider in the assessment of the claim of a family member. They are:

1.   the services must replace services that were necessary for your care;
2.   the services have to be over and above what would be expected from the marital or family relationship;
3.   the amount of compensation should reflect its true and reasonable value.

A judge recently concluded the following in a case of a seriously injured woman:
"I find that… Mr. B performed numerous services that can properly be said to be nursing or attendant care services necessary for the care of Mrs. B. Further, I find these services to be substantially over and above what would be expected from the marital relationship."
"I accept, however, that… there were times… when Mr. B was not providing services in the form of actual care or otherwise, or alternatively, when what services he did perform did not go beyond the normal duties flowing from a husband / wife relationship and are therefore not compensable." He then made an "in trust" award based on 70% of the hours the husband claimed at an hourly rate of 75% of what a health care company charged for the services of a health care attendant.

Q: My husband has suffered a great deal as a result of my injuries. Is he entitled to compensation for how his life has changed? He has to put up with me being in pain and we cannot do many of the activities we enjoyed together before the collision?

A: Your husband's loss is real and substantial. However our courts take a much more conservative approach than the courts south of the border on this issue. They do not compensate people for their loss of enjoyment of life resulting from the injuries to a member of their family.

CHAPTER 15

VALUING DAMAGES: LOSS OF INCOME

Q: I lost the chance to earn more money after my collision than I earned before the collision. Am I entitled to be compensated for this?
A: Yes, if you can prove that there is a real possibility (more than speculation) that you would have earned more money after the collision than you earned before the collision. However your loss must be discounted to take into account the less than 100% chance that you would have earned this additional income.

A B.C. Court of Appeal justice wrote: "While past work history is not determinative of what will occur in the future, it is a significant factor to consider when estimating the likelihood of what would have happened in the future but for the accident." Therefore you will need solid evidence to support this claim. Such evidence can vary greatly. It can include the evidence of employers about your work performance prior to the accident and opportunities you missed after the accident and the evidence of an economist on the job opportunities and average incomes in your field.

Q: ICBC wants to reduce my loss of income claim by 30% for taxes I would have paid. Is this the law? If I have to pay tax on my settlement or court award this would be double taxation.
A: The ICBC regulations say that past (not future) loss of income must be calculated on the injured person's **net** loss of income after deduction for taxes and EI premiums. Judges have interpreted this to mean that the amount of taxes to be deducted is based on your entire loss of income having been earned in the year before the court makes its award.

As an example, if you lost $125,000 in gross income over a four year period before you went to court the judge will reduce this loss by the tax and EI premiums you would have paid on income of $125,000 in the year before the trial. This is in contrast to the reduction being your tax on the amount you lost in each of the four years.

Each year economists provide lawyers and ICBC with tables of tax and EI premiums to be deducted from various amounts of income.

If your loss of income is only $10,000 or $20,000 the reduction for taxes and EI should be very low.

Q: I was forced to collect EI sickness benefits and then social assistance when I was unable to return to work after my collision. Is ICBC entitled by law to deduct these benefits from my loss of income claim?
A: The law does not allow ICBC to deduct the amount you received in EI sickness benefits from your claim for loss of income. That is because you paid part of your EI premiums.

The Supreme Court of Canada recently changed the law regarding welfare payments. ICBC is now entitled to deduct these payments from your loss of income claim.

If EI insisted you sign an agreement to repay the sickness benefits you receive out of your settlement or court award you should seek legal advice as to whether or not you have to repay EI and, if so, how much.

Q: I am self employed. How is my past loss of income calculated?

A: The most important documents in proving your loss of income are your tax returns for a few years before the collision. They show the trend over the years in your gross revenue. They also show the percentage of your total income you spent on various business expenses. If you did not declare all your income it will be difficult, but not impossible, to show that your income was higher than you declared it to be.

Your loss of income can be assessed as follows:

1.   the revenue you lost since the collision, considering the trend in your revenue before the collision and considering changing economic conditions before and after the collision,
2.   plus the additional labour expenses you incurred to make up for your reduced ability to contribute to your business,
3.   less the "variable expenses" you saved as a result of your reduced revenue. These are expenses that vary with the amount of the revenue of your business. They include the costs of bookkeeping, operating your vehicle, long distance telephone calls, office supplies, the input cost of goods you produce and, in the case of construction businesses, the cost of building materials.
4.   less taxes on your net loss of income.

For example, if you lost revenue of $100,000 since the collision and in the three years before the collision your variable expenses averaged 27% of your revenue your loss of income would be $100,000 less $27,000 in variable expenses you saved plus additional labour expenses you incurred less taxes.

Sometimes the accountant your business uses may be able to prepare a report calculating your lost income. However frequently this is outside their area of expertise. Lawyers often hire accountants or business valuators who are trained and certified in quantifying business losses for legal purposes.

CHAPTER 16

VALUING DAMAGES:
LOSS OF FUTURE EARNING CAPACITY

Q: What questions do the court and ICBC ask when they are valuing the loss of future earning capacity of an injured person?
A: In determining the loss of future earning capacity of an injured person, judges and juries ask themselves the following questions:
- Is he/she less capable overall from earning income from all types of employment?
- Is he/she less marketable?
- Has he/she lost ability to take advantage of all job opportunities that might otherwise have been open to him/her?
- Is he/she less valuable to himself as a person capable of earning income in a competitive labour market?

The court will also ask itself what the difference will be between:
- the value of the future income flow of the injured person had he/she never been injured, and
- its reduced value as a result of the collision.

During negotiations, both ICBC and your lawyer will consider how the courts value these claims.

You do not have to prove that there is a greater than 50% chance (that it is more likely than not) that you will suffer a loss of income in the future. You just have to prove there is a "real possibility" that you will lose income in the future. In its award, the court must consider the degree of possibility of your future income loss. It may conclude, for example, that you should be compensated for a 5% chance of future income loss.

The court must also take into account the uncertainties of your income if the collision had **never** occurred and of any **increased** uncertainties as a result of the collision. For example, had the collision never happened:
- You may have experienced the average rate of unemployment of your occupation. For example, teachers have a much lower average unemployment rate than do construction workers;
- You may also have retired earlier than age 65 due to illness or due your own choice, or you may have chosen to work beyond age 65;
- You were largely protected from the uncertainty of ill health by your employer's contribution to your benefits package including disability insurance.

Now your chances of a reduced wages for each hour you work and also of unemployment and early retirement due to your injury may be much higher. These chances are not easy to quantify except in the case of injured people who clearly will never be able to work again. In many cases, economists provide statistics on these chances, which are called "labour market contingencies." They also provide statistics based on census data and surveys on the average income over time of a full-time worker in a particular occupation and educational level.

These statistics allow a judge or jury to more accurately value a person's lost earning capacity. You may be able to prove that you would have earned a more-than-average wage for your occupation or educational level based on your pre-accident track record.

While the facts of some cases lend themselves more readily to the application of statistical and mathematical evidence in the assessment process than do those of other cases, the Court of Appeal has made it clear that valuing future loss of income is not purely an arithmetical exercise. The most important question is whether the award is "fair and adequate" to compensate the injured person for his or her lost future capacity to earn income. Of course, this is a fairly vague concept unless one bases it on at least some mathematics.

Q: I have to retrain for a less physically demanding job than the one I did before the collision. It also pays less. How do I prove the value of my lost future income?
A: While physical impairments generally have a greater financial impact on people who use their bodies for their work, limitations in the ability to sit and work at a computer much of the work day can also impair a person's earning capacity.

First, you have to prove you cannot handle your job and what jobs you are now able to handle. Family physicians have few tools at their disposal that allow them to give a strong opinion on your physical limitations unless they are very obvious. General practitioners will often rely heavily on what their patients tell them. This rarely holds water in a legal case.

Occupational therapists with special training may evaluate your present ability to function at work by doing an assessment that takes between four hours and two days; however, they are not qualified to predict your future. For more information on this, see Chapter 19.

You will need a top medical specialist to predict whether your present work limitations will improve, remain about the same or deteriorate in the future in the short, medium and long term, and to what degree. This is generally a very difficult task.

ICBC will no doubt hire one of its frequently used medical specialists to do an assessment. These specialists tend to minimize the effect of your injuries on your life and to be optimistic about your future, so it is imperative that you obtain the opinion of a medical specialist who has plenty of legal experience and who has proven that he or she will hold up well in court in the event that your case proceeds to trial. When ICBC negotiates settlements, it considers which expert's opinion is most likely to be accepted by the court.

Your former supervisors, employers and even teachers can provide very powerful evidence as to your potential for advancement in your occupation as of the day before you were injured.

You may also need a vocational rehabilitation consultant to consider the medical opinions on your physical or mental limitations and to explain how your limitations will impact your ability to earn a living. Which occupations that were formerly open to you are now closed to you? How difficult will it be for you to obtain and retain work now? ICBC may hire a vocational consultant who tends to be very optimistic about the vocational future of injured people, so you will need a top-notch consultant.

You may also need a labour market economist to place a monetary value on the difference between your possible and probable future income flows both:
• had you not been injured, and
• as a result of your injuries.

The combination of the opinions of your work capacity evaluator, medical specialist, vocational consultant and economist will enable your lawyer to place a value on your loss of earning capacity for the purposes of settlement negotiations and, if necessary, for court.

Q: I am worried that I will not be able to work full-time or at all when I am in my 50's and 60's due to post-traumatic osteoarthritis in my neck and left knee. How do I prove my claim?
A: Post-traumatic osteoarthritis causes degenerative change in the surface of a joint resulting from acceleration of normal wear and tear. There are joints in your spine, just as there is in your knee.

Injury to a joint surface can damage the articular cartilage. Injuries to a ligament can make the joint unstable. Significant damage to supporting muscles can lead to inadequate joint stability and premature wear and tear of the articular cartilage.

Medical specialists will determine the likelihood that you will develop post-traumatic arthritis based on such factors as:
• the mechanism and location of the injury,
• your particular complaints,
• signs on examination such as loss of movement and stiffness or fluid on the joint,
• x-ray results - these may not show up until a few years after the injury,
• bone scans - these may show inflammation in a joint after the usual healing would be expected to be complete, and
• arthroscopy of the knee, shoulder, elbow or ankle.

Rheumatologists' advantage in the legal system is that they are the specialists who see patients with post-traumatic arthritis many years after they have injured a joint. They do not perform arthroscopy but may refer a patient to an orthopaedic surgeon for this procedure if they think it would be of value.

Some **orthopaedic surgeons** are good experts on this issue, but an inordinate number tend to be on the optimistic side. Before you see an orthopaedic surgeon, check with an injury lawyer to find out if the surgeon has any strong biases.

Your specialist may recommend an expensive brace that may require relatively frequent replacement. This expense would become part of your cost of future care claim.

The specialist may provide an opinion on the likelihood that your condition will advance to the point where you may need a fusion of your injured joint or a total joint replacement (which lasts only ten to fifteen years). He or she may also provide an opinion on the likelihood that you will not be able to continue with your present job or other physically demanding jobs when you are 50, 55 and 60 years old.

You then may need the opinion of a **vocational consultant** on your ability to change occupations now or in the future and the effect this may have on your income. Your future financial loss may be greater if you do not have the ability to move to a less physically demanding job that pays as well as your present job.

You may also need the opinion of an **economist** on the present value of income you may lose ten and twenty years from now. Your future income loss is discounted by the courts - and, therefore, by ICBC - to present value. This is based on the court's assumption that you will be able to gain a return on your invested award that is higher than the rate of inflation, and that wages will increase faster than the rate of inflation.

In summary, experts in the field of rheumatology, vocational rehabilitation and economics may be able to help you prove your future damages caused by post-traumatic arthritis.

Q: I was a student when I was seriously injured and can no longer do mentally challenging jobs. How do I prove the value of my lost future earning capacity when I don't have a track record?
A: Please see the answers to the first two questions in this chapter to get a sense of the general principles governing claims for loss of future earning capacity.

You have raised two issues. Firstly, what is the value of your earning potential had the collision never occurred? Secondly, what is the value of your earning potential now? Your loss of future earning capacity is the difference between the two.

First, let's look at **your earning potential absent the collision.** In order to value this, the court will place a great emphasis on the likelihood that you would have achieved various educational levels had you not been injured. The courts do this because there is a strong proven correlation between a person's educational level and income over his or her working life. For example, on average, women with university degrees earn more over their lifetimes than do women with 2-year college diplomas even though they start their careers two years later.

Important evidence to establish the chances that you would have attained various educational levels would be your:

- school marks before the collision,
- IQ before the collision if you were tested,
- former teachers' evidence about your intelligence, work habits and ambition,
- father's educational level (because there is a proven relationship between the educational achievement of a father and his children),
- stated ambitions and the steps you had taken to realize your ambitions before the collision.

If you had already chosen a career path and you were far enough along in your education, the court may rely on summaries from a labour economist of census data on the average full-time incomes over time (in 5 year increments) in that particular career or occupation and then consider average rates from an economist of unemployment, part-time work and withdrawal from the workforce over time. It would be challenging to persuade a court that you would have earned more or less than average as your career progressed, other than in exceptional circumstances.

If you are a young woman, it is crucial to try to establish that average incomes over time for males rather than females are the appropriate figures to apply to you. If, however, your evidence is that you intended to have children and stay home with them for several years, you will likely have some difficulty persuading a court to use male average incomes.

I discussed above how a court will view certain evidence rather than how ICBC will view it - in spite of the fact that most cases settle without a trial. Before ICBC negotiates with you, however, it will carefully consider how a court will likely look at your case.

The second issue is **proving your future income as a result of the collision**. You will likely need to be tested by a neuropsychologist if you suffered a head injury or even have chronic pain. He or she will interview you and a close friend or relative, administer psychological tests and perform assessments to determine the extent of your problems with thinking, emotions and behaviour.

You will also likely need to be tested by a vocational rehabilitation consultant. He or she will interview you and administer tests of your interests and of various skills that are needed in various jobs. The consultant will then recommend jobs he or she thinks you would be capable of performing even part-time. He or she may give you options for retraining. Another type of vocational rehabilitation consultant will help find a job placement for you, observe how you do in the real world and report on his or her findings.

Lawyers hire all three of these experts (labour economists, neuropsychologist and vocational rehab experts) in order to assist their clients to maximize their potential and to prove the extent of their limitations.

Q: I can no longer do my former job due to my injuries. My employer gave me a lighter job at the same rate of pay. Do I have a claim for lost future earning capacity?

A: The British Columbia Court of Appeal stated the following in a leading case called *Palmer v. Goodall*:

> "Because it is impairment that is being redressed, **even a plaintiff who is apparently going to be able to earn as much** as he could have earned if not injured or who, with retraining, on the balance of probabilities will be able to do so, is entitled to some compensation for the impairment. He is entitled to it because for the rest of his life some occupations will be closed to him and it is impossible to say that over his working life the impairment will not harm his income earning ability."

It is important to go back to fundamentals. Are you:

*   less capable overall from earning income from all types of employment?
*   less marketable?
*   less valuable to yourself as a person capable of earning income in a competitive labour market?

Have you lost ability to take advantage of all job opportunities that might otherwise have been open to you?

If so, you may have a claim for loss of future earning capacity even though you have not yet lost any income due to your injuries since your initial period of disability.

The British Columbia Court of Appeal stated the following in the equally leading case of *Pallos v. ICBC*:

> "The cases to which we were referred suggest **various means of assigning a dollar value to the loss of capacity to earn income**. One method is to postulate a minimum annual income loss for the plaintiff's remaining years of work, to multiply the annual projected loss times the number of years remaining, and to calculate a present value of this sum. Another is to award the present value of some nominal percentage loss per annum applied against the plaintiff's expected annual income. In the end, all of these methods seem equally arbitrary. It has, however, often been said that the difficulty of making a fair assessment of damages cannot relieve the court of its duty to do so."

In Pallos, the Court of Appeal held that $40,000 was a fair amount for lost future earning capacity. Mr. Pallos was a labourer who suffered a leg injury resulting in permanent pain. After his accident, he could not do heavy lifting and was restricted to lighter duties and work that did not require him to climb ladders or stairs. He returned to work and earned more after the accident than he had prior to it.

It is important to obtain legal advice on this complex issue. There is clearly no mathematical formula that can be used in these cases to arrive at a damages award, but the annual income of the injured person is certainly a consideration.

Q: What is the effect of taxation on my claim for loss of future earning capacity?
A: Courts must consider the effect of taxation in awards for past loss of income, but they are not to consider the effect of taxation on awards for loss of future earning capacity.

Q: What is the effect of my receiving Long Term Disability (LTD) and Canada Pension Plan disability benefits on my claim for loss of future earning capacity?
A: The courts are to ignore the facts that you will be receiving these monthly benefits in the future from your disability insurer or from CPP, so this will not reduce your claim.

Your entitlement to damages may be reduced, however, if your claim is under:
• "Underinsured Motorist" coverage due to the wrongdoer having insufficient third party liability insurance, or
• "Unidentified Motorist" coverage in the case of a hit and run collision.

You should seek legal advice on what deductions may be made if you have either of these claims.

Q: As a young woman, I don't think it is fair that the value of the future earning potential I had before my injury should be compared to that of women who are now in their 50's and 60's. Times have changed. Can I avoid this?
A: It is very much in your best interests if the value of your future earning capacity absent the collision is compared to that of men - not women. This is because the average income of women in most occupations is lower than that of men. This can be partly attributed to the times women stop working or work part-time while they raise their children. It can also be partly attributed to the fact that the percentage of women who continue to work after their mid-fifties rapidly drops off.

Your lawyer's challenge is to persuade ICBC and, if necessary, the court that your working life will be very different from that of average women now in their 50's. This is due to the likelihood that you will take much less time off work if and when you have children and the likelihood that you will not retire until between ages 62 and 65. You will have a stronger argument on the second point if you are married and your husband is not more than one or two years older than you.

Q: Is my loss of future income calculated to age 65?
A: Compensation in our legal system is not "one size fits all." It is individually designed based on the inherent worth of each person and the evidence in each case. The court's object is to put the injured person in as close a position financially to where he or she would have been had no collision occurred.

Your loss of future income will not be calculated to exactly age 65 unless ICBC - or, failing settlement, the court - concludes that it is a virtual certainty that you would have worked to age 65 had your collision not occurred. If, for example, you would have received maximum pension benefits at age 62 had you not been injured, it is unlikely that a court will conclude that you would have worked past age 62 unless there was very strong evidence to show you would have continued working.

On the other hand, a court may calculate your loss of income up to age 70 if, for example, you:
- had only $120,000 in retirement savings when you were injured at age 60,
- had only a small pension plan,
- were passionate about your work,
- had few hobbies or sports you loved to spend a lot of time on, and
- told one or more credible people before your collision that you intended to continue to work until age 70.

The court, however, would most likely reduce your award for loss of future income to account for the possibility that:
- you would become unable to work to age 70 due to ill health,
- you would be become unemployed against your will, and
- you would have changed your mind and chosen to stop working before age 70.

Labour economists provide evidence of census information on the average retirement date of men and women in British Columbia and the likelihood that men and women of a certain age range are not "participating" in the work force. On average, women retire earlier than men. One likely reason is that, on average, their husbands are a few years older than they are.

Q: Do I have to retrain for another line of work if I can no longer do the job I enjoyed and was good at? It isn't my fault that I can't do my job.
A: Our legal system does not compel an injured person to retrain or to work. If you choose to not retrain or to find alternative work that you can handle, however, the court will award you damages for loss of future earning capacity based on the assumption that you took all reasonable steps to mitigate (minimize) your losses. This may well involve at least some retraining.

The British Columbia Court of Appeal said the following in the case of *Parypa v. Wickware*:
> "...the plaintiff is not entitled to compensation based solely on the type of work she was performing at the time of the accident. There is a duty on the plaintiff to mitigate her damages by seeking, if at all possible, a line of work that can be pursued in spite of her injuries. If the plaintiff is unqualified for such work, then she is required, within the limits of her abilities, to pursue education or training that would qualify her for such work."

Another factor to consider is that judges, juries and ICBC adjusters are most impressed by injured people who never give up and make every effort to overcome their adversity in spite of the odds against them. Such injured people usually receive larger settlements or court awards.

CHAPTER 17

WHAT YOU NEED FROM MEDICAL EXPERTS
TO PROVE YOUR CLAIM

Q: My family doctor does not seem to have the time to examine me. Is this a problem?
A: Yes. A family doctor is trained to accept what a patient says at face value. This may well be standard practice for the treatment of many diseases. Your situation is now different because you are claiming compensation for your injuries. ICBC will give no credence to a report from your doctor that simply recites what you told him or her. ICBC and the courts want "objective evidence" of your limitations - evidence that is not reliant on what you say or do. An x-ray, CT scan or MRI scan showing your injury is strong objective evidence. Unfortunately, many injuries to ligaments, tendons and muscles do not show up in these scans; therefore, the results of physical examinations over time by your family doctor are important objective evidence of your injury.

Q: How frequently should I see my family doctor from a legal perspective?
A: Ask your doctor at the end of each appointment when he thinks it best that you see him again. From a legal perspective, you should see you doctor every month or so during the first six to twelve months and then every two months or so while you continue to experience pain and limitations.

There is little or no value from a legal perspective in you seeing your doctor unless he **examines** you when you see him or her. Some family doctors examine their injured patients monthly. Others examine their injured patients rarely, or perhaps only once soon after their accident and never again. If your doctor is in the latter group, your challenge is to assertively persuade him or her to examine you every 3 to 5 weeks, at least during the first 6 to 12 months, and then every second month from then on if you continue to experience pain and limitations.

Q: Who else can give me examination results that will support my injury claim?
A: Physiotherapists are well trained in physically testing for injuries, and they generally do the testing fairly regularly to monitor your progress. If you cannot persuade your family doctor to examine you, or if his examination is very cursory, inform your physiotherapist of this and ask if he or she would mind recording examination results regularly and writing a "medico-legal" report for you once you are doing better. A physiotherapist expects to be paid for preparing this report. Most lawyers pay for physiotherapists' reports and usually recover this cost from ICBC as part of your settlement or court award.

Chiropractors and massage therapists will also provide reports that disclose their physical findings.

Q: Who is best able to help me prove that I am not able to work full-time or to do all my household and garden chores or return to my sports?

A: Physicians, physiotherapists and chiropractors can be very useful in treating you and in showing that there is a physical "objective" basis for your pain; however, many of the leading specialists will openly admit that it is very difficult to accurately conclude from an office examination how well you are able to function in the real world with real physical demands. Drawing these conclusions becomes increasingly more difficult over time because your physical signs generally become less obvious over time. For example, your muscle spasms may have gradually resolved after a month or two, yet you continue to have a lot of pain with certain movements. At some point, you will need someone else to objectively support your ongoing pain and limitations. That person is usually a certified work capacity evaluator. (see Chapter 19).

CHAPTER 18

MEDICAL SPECIALISTS: REFERRED BY YOUR DOCTOR
OR BY ICBC OR BY YOUR LAWYER

Q: ICBC has asked me to see a doctor they have chosen. Do I have to go?
A: This is an extremely important question because ICBC pays a handful of selected doctors between $200,000 and $796,000 each per year. These doctors' opinions about your injuries and degree of disability are generally on the "conservative" side, whereas their opinions about your future possible problems tend to be on the "optimistic" side.

ICBC will try to convince you to visit a doctor of its choice. As lawyers, our objectives are:
- to ensure our clients avoid these "defence medical examinations", or
- to at least avoid allowing ICBC to rely on the opinions of the doctors they choose in court.

To maximize your chances of success, you should seek legal advice for this part of your case as soon as ICBC asks you to visit a doctor of its choice. You do not necessarily have to decide to hire a lawyer for your entire case at that time. You may ask a lawyer to deal with this issue alone. Our firm and others offer free initial consultations in the types of cases we handle.

Q: What do I need to know before I agree to see a medical specialist that my family doctor has referred me to?
A: Some specialists are very skilled, experienced and interested in dealing with medico-legal issues and their opinions hold up very well in negotiations with ICBC and, if necessary, in court. An injured person with an ICBC claim should try to avoid specialists who do not have these qualities.

Some specialists are very conservative in their views of injuries, whereas others:
- may be used a great deal by ICBC,
- are quick to impute exaggeration,
- may have a reputation with ICBC or the courts as an "advocate" for either ICBC or injured people and thus lack credibility,
- may not be keeping up with the latest ever-changing scientific knowledge in their field,
- may hate to write medico-legal reports for lawyers,
- may write poor reports,
- may be much more optimistic about people's futures than most specialists in their field.

If your doctor is considering referring you to a specialist, talk to an experienced injury lawyer about this as soon as possible. From a legal as well as medical standpoint, it is important that you see only top-notch specialists who don't have the negative qualities mentioned above. Unfortunately, these top-notch specialists often have longer waiting lists. Some specialists reserve blocks of time to assess people referred by lawyers. This might get you in quicker.

Specialists always write the family doctor a report after a referred patient's first or second appointment. It is virtually impossible to hide an unfavourable report on you from a specialist to your family doctor. If you go to court and do not give the court the report from a particular doctor who has treated you, the court is entitled to conclude that this doctor had something negative to say about you. This rule can hurt you not only in court but also when negotiating with ICBC. ICBC is entitled to obtain copies of the negative reports the specialist wrote to your family doctor and will argue that even your own treating specialist, whom your family doctor entrusted to treat you, agreed with ICBC's doctor about the lack of severity of your injury and your bright future.

Lawyers for injured people often hire top specialists to assess their injured clients and give them opinions for injury claims. We claim reimbursement of this cost from ICBC on completion of the case.

CHAPTER 19

WORK CAPACITY EVALUATORS

Q: Is there a profession dedicated to measuring injured people's physical limitations?
A: Yes. Specially trained occupational therapists (O.T.s) called certified work capacity evaluators spend a minimum of 4 hours testing how an injured person is able to function. The assessment is called a functional capacity evaluation (FCE). These therapists sometimes visit a patient's house and garden or place of work to see what the patient's demands are and how he or she is doing. This is a very powerful tool in proving your case. In your case, the O.T. may conclude:

- you showed your maximum abilities at present during testing,
- you can or cannot handle sedentary, light, medium or heavy work or chores and for how long,
- the pain levels you reported during the assessment are likely true (the medical profession has no tool yet to measure pain; therefore, this is likely as close as we can now come to proving a person's pain),
- the number of hours per day and days per week you can work,
- the job, household chores and sports you can handle,
- what ergonomic changes would help you at work,
- how many hours per week of assistance you need with your heavier household chores and with your garden chores,
- you would benefit from certain rehabilitation that you have not yet received in order to improve your ability to function, or
- it is unlikely that further rehabilitation will make much difference in your level of functioning at work and at home, and that you should find another line of work.

Even if a family doctor's standard examination shows very little, this type of testing could still show very significant ongoing limitations. For example, one test compares your floor-to-shoulder lifting strength to that of thousands of others across North America of your same sex, age, weight and height. Let's say your strength on this test is at the 10th percentile for your age. This means that on this test, 90% of men your age are stronger than you. This is powerful evidence if, for example, you were a house framer and an avid hockey player before the accident and you have not returned to either activity. It can also provide equally powerful evidence for women.

Q: Who pays for this evaluation?
A: This O.T. evaluation is not covered by your regular B.C. medical insurance (MSP) or extended health plan. People's lawyers pay for this testing in almost every case. We later request reimbursement of these fees from ICBC when a client's case is resolved.

Q: My job involves sitting at a desk all day and working on a computer. My doctor has advised me to work as many hours per day as I feel I can. If I follow this advice, will it support my wage loss claim with ICBC?

A: From a legal perspective, this is very weak advice and will likely not support a wage loss claim. When your body maintains one position for an extended period it is called "static loading." This is in contrast to "intermittent loading," which occurs when your body is moving. It is well accepted medically that many people with neck and back injuries have far more difficulty with static loading than with intermittent loading. Many physiotherapists recommend that people with office jobs take frequent breaks to stretch and move around.

Because most doctors have great difficulty determining how many hours per day patients with these problems are able to work, they advise their patients that it is up to them to decide. In claiming damages for your loss of income and pain and suffering, a medical opinion on how much you can work is much stronger than **you** saying that you can only work 4 hours per day before the pain becomes intolerable.

You may benefit from testing by a functional capacity evaluator, who is likely an occupational therapist. He or she will probably need a day or two to evaluate you in his or her office to reach a conclusion regarding your maximum work capacity. He or she may also go to your office to ensure that your office set-up is ergonomically correct. After such an assessment, the evaluator should be able to come up with a solid opinion on your limitations at work, at home and recreationally, and give you recommendations on improving the ergonomics of your worksite.

CHAPTER 20

HIRING A LAWYER: AVOIDING THE PITFALLS

Q: How do I find out which lawyer in my community is the best for my case?
A: Many lawyers advertise for personal injury cases, but only some are very experienced in this field. Some of these lawyers have so many small cases in their offices that few cases get their personal attention. Others have no real intention of trying your case themselves, and if the case can't be settled with ICBC, they will refer the case out for a trial.

Separating the good lawyers from others can be difficult, so I've put together a few questions you can ask and things to look for that will lead you to the best person for your case, no matter what type of claim you may have. Not every lawyer will meet all the criteria, but a low rating on an item should be a warning sign.

• **Experience.** Obviously, the longer a lawyer has been practicing a particular area of the law, the more he or she will know. Experience is a big factor in most cases.

• **Experience trying cases.** Ask the lawyer how many cases he has actually tried. Has he or she achieved any significant verdicts or settlements? Does he/she have a list of verdicts and settlements available that you can review? Don't accept the "All my cases are confidential" line! The greater the number of cases he/she has tried and the more substantial verdicts and settlements he/she has achieved, the more likely ICBC will respect him/her. Past results don't necessarily guarantee the future but they illustrate the level of experience and success.

• **Respect in the legal community.** Does the lawyer teach in his area of expertise?

• **Membership in trial lawyer associations.** Is the lawyer a member of the Trial Lawyers Association of BC?

• Does the law firm also **represent ICBC?**

Before you walk in the door, ask each lawyer if he or she has a website or written material where you can learn more about their qualifications, experience and method of handling a case.

Be wary about any lawyer who rushes you into signing a contingency (percentage) fee agreement.

Q: Do I really need a lawyer to settle my case?
A: You definitely don't need a lawyer for every small injury case. In fact, our office doesn't even accept cases where there's little or no property damage or the injuries are

minor. However, for more severe injury claims it's wise to get a lawyer involved early on.

Q: Will I risk receiving less help from ICBC early on if I hire a lawyer?
A: This depends upon your specific case. If you are seriously injured and are dealing with Head Office Claims or ICBC's Rehabilitation Department, ICBC will most likely treat you the same way, whether you have a lawyer or not. If you are dealing with a local claim centre, it is possible that ICBC will not pay you money in the short term over and above what it owes you under your Accident Benefits if you hire a lawyer. From ICBC's perspective, the longer the adjuster can deter you from hiring a lawyer, the more control it has over you and your claim and the more chance it will find weaknesses in your claim.
This doesn't mean you shouldn't obtain initial legal advice, which is usually free. It just means that you and your lawyer need to decide if it's in your best interests to advise ICBC that you have retained a lawyer. It may be better for you to wait until you decide that you won't suffer financially in the short term before you agree that your lawyer contact ICBC on your behalf.

Q: When is the best time to hire a lawyer to handle my case?
A: There's a big difference between obtaining initial legal advice and formally hiring a lawyer. It never hurts to obtain initial legal advice early on so you know your rights and what to watch out for.

The best time to actually hire a lawyer depends on a number of factors. If you are seriously injured or if you are possibly at fault in the accident, you should seek legal advice immediately. After discussing your case in detail with a lawyer, you may decide to wait before actually hiring a lawyer, or to hire a lawyer and wait awhile before he or she contacts ICBC.

You may decide that it would be valuable to have your lawyer **hire** as soon as possible an **accident reconstruction engineer** to:
- examine the vehicles before they are repaired or destroyed,
- search for debris from the vehicles at the accident scene, and
- examine skid marks at the accident scene before they disappear.

You may also decide to have someone other than **ICBC interview each of the witnesses** to the accident as soon as possible. We use private investigators or former adjusters or we speak to them ourselves.

The lawyer will advise you exactly:
- what you should expect from ICBC in the short term regarding income replacement, rehabilitation, household help and home care,
- what you should do and avoid doing to ensure you have the strongest possible case in the long term,
- what medical experts would be valuable in terms of both your rehabilitation and in proving your case,

47

- when it would be in your best interest to commence a legal action (sue the other driver).

Q: Do percentage fees vary?
A: Percentage or contingency fee agreements vary between law firms, as does the quality of service and the time lawyers spend on a case.

Some lawyers charge a flat percentage fee, no matter when the case is resolved. Others charge fees that increase, depending upon whether the case is settled:
- before an examination for discovery (pre-court questioning under oath),
- after an examination for discovery and more than a certain number of days before trial, and
- if the case proceeds to trial, or if it is settled less than a certain number of days before the trial.

Fee rates vary depending upon the severity of the client's injury and the amount of risk involved in the case. There is much competition in fees for seriously injured clients.

Lawyers are not permitted to charge more than 33.33% of damages recovered in ICBC claims unless a Supreme Court judge pre-approves the fee agreement. A judge may approve a higher fee if a case is particularly risky.

Q: If I hire a lawyer, who pays the expenses to fight my case such as the cost of expert reports?
A: Most lawyers who focus their practice on injury cases agree to pay the expenses of fighting the case because most injured people can't afford to pay these expenses. These expenses become part of your final claim against ICBC for damages and "costs." Most lawyers charge interest on these expenses. Interest rates vary greatly. Some lawyers charge interest of 15%, 18% per annum, or even more. Ask yourself if this is reasonable, considering the low cost of borrowing money today and the very high likelihood that the lawyer will be repaid when your case resolves if you are not at fault.

Q: How do legal fees work if I change lawyers?
A: If you are not satisfied with your lawyer's services, you are free to change lawyers. Before you fire your lawyer, however, obtain a second opinion from the lawyer you are thinking of hiring to determine if it is economically viable for you to change lawyers. Unless your first lawyer does an incompetent job in handling a case, or was unethical she will be entitled to some fee at the end of your case (but not earlier) for the services provided.

The amount of this fee depends in part upon the terms of the fee contract. Some contingency fee agreements state that the lawyer is entitled to a fee at a certain hourly rate if the client fires the lawyer. Other agreements state that the lawyer is entitled to a reasonable fee for services rendered.

A number of factors are considered in determining a reasonable fee after termination. These include:
- the time the lawyer spent,
- the quality of the services the lawyer provided, and
- the lawyer's standing in the legal profession.

If you cannot resolve your differences with your lawyer or if you have completely lost confidence in him/her, it may make economic sense to change lawyers. In smaller cases, however, it may not make economic sense.

Q: Is there any harm in my hiring a member of a law firm who also does work for ICBC?
A: Several law firms across the province work for ICBC and also for injured people.
If a law firm wants to work for ICBC, it must sign what ICBC calls a "strategic alliance" agreement with ICBC. In this agreement, all members of the firm must agree to not claim punitive or aggravated damages against ICBC on behalf of their injured clients or to claim that ICBC has acted in bad faith towards their injured clients.

ICBC is your insurer for your Accident Benefits (disability and rehabilitation benefits). The law imposes on it a duty to act in the utmost of good faith towards you regarding your Accident Benefits. What if ICBC acts in bad faith towards you after you have hired your lawyer? Will your lawyer be able to sue ICBC for bad faith, or at least threaten to do so if ICBC does not reinstate your Accident Benefits? The conduct of the person who injured you may give you the right to claim aggravated or punitive damages against him. Will your lawyer be able to bring such a claim on your behalf, considering his firm's agreement with ICBC?

The Law Society of B.C. requires that lawyers whose firms enter into these agreements with ICBC must advise their clients of their relationship with ICBC, the restrictions on the lawyers and the implications of those restrictions.

Ask yourself if there is a possible conflict of interest if a lawyer represents you when his firm has entered into this restrictive agreement with ICBC. Is it possible that the lawyer may be even tempted to soft pedal parts of your claim?

Q: Can I rely on the Yellow Pages and lawyer referral service?
A: There are four things you should remember about the **Yellow Pages**:
- Many top lawyers don't advertise in the Yellow Pages. Most of their cases come from referrals from other lawyers and medical people, or from satisfied clients.
- Be careful about the ads that tout too many different specialities. No one can do everything well.
- Be careful about the double-page and full-page ads. This advertising typically attracts a lot of minor cases that can overwhelm a lawyer. Make sure the lawyer you hire is selective

enough with his or her cases that your important case doesn't become just one more file in the pile.

- You should never hire a lawyer based solely on advertising - anyone can buy a slick commercial!

The Canadian Bar Association has a **lawyer referral service**. Lawyers sign up under certain specialties and their names come up on a rotating basis. Keep in mind that these lawyers do not have to prove their qualifications to be placed on this list.

There are some lawyer referral sites on the internet. Lawyers pay to be on these sites.

Q: What does your firm offer clients that would really help me?
A: We are "different".

We don't rely on a high volume of cases. Each year, we accept a limited number of injury cases from the hundreds of people who ask us to represent them. We are not a "TV advertising personal injury mill." We do not allow paralegals and assistants to negotiate your case with ICBC or your disability insurance company. Fewer cases means more time for you and, we believe, better results overall.

If your case passes our test and we accept it, you can be assured that you will receive personal attention. We will aggressively represent you, keep you up to date on what is happening in your case, and give you advice as to whether you should settle your case or go to trial.

We will fully explain all fees and costs to you before we start working on your case. Together, as a team, we will decide on the best tactics for your case.

If you would like to see the awards we have been getting for our clients, I invite you to go to our website at www.icbcinjurylawyers.ca. and click on "outstanding results."

CHAPTER 21

A PERSONAL INJURY LAWSUIT AGAINST ICBC

Q: Do I have to start a lawsuit within a certain period of time after my accident?
You must sue within two years, or your claim ceases to exist. Two exceptions to this rule are if the injured person is:
- under nineteen years of age, or
- mentally incompetent.

When someone under nineteen is injured in an accident, he or she must sue within two years of turning nineteen. If, however, the guardian of that person receives a written notice that the two-year limitation period has begun and the notice meets the requirements of the Limitation Act of B.C., the two years begins from the date the notice was delivered.

If a person is incapable of, or substantially impeded in, managing his or her affairs, then the two-year limitation does not begin until the person ceases to be under this disability.

Q: What are the steps in a personal injury lawsuit?
A: Here is a more or less complete list of the tasks a lawyer may be called to do in your case. Remember that each case is different, and that not all of these tasks will be required in every case. They are:

- Initial interview with the client.
- Educate the client about personal injury claims.
- Gather documentary evidence including police accident reports, medical records and bills.
- Interview known witnesses.
- Collect other evidence, such as photographs of the vehicles and the accident scene.
- Analyze the legal issues, such as contributory negligence and damages.
- Obtain records from the client's physicians in order to fully understand the client's condition.
- Obtain records from the client's employer, disability insurer, if they have one, and from WorkSafeBC BC, if they have had any claims.
- Analyze the client's disability policy to ascertain whether any money they paid to the client must be repaid.
- Decide with the client whether an attempt will be made to negotiate the case with ICBC or whether a law suit shall be filed.
- If a law suit is filed, prepare the client for questioning at the examination for discovery and accompany the client to their discovery.
- Apply to the court to set a trial date.
- Prepare for and attend a mediation or settlement conference.
- Prepare the client and witnesses for trial.

51

- Ensure the client has the best possible medical and income loss evidence for negotiations and trial.
- Organize the preparation of medical reports for trial.
- Organize the preparation of demonstrative exhibits for trial.
- Take the case to trial with a jury or judge in the event that a fair settlement cannot be reached.

Once a lawsuit is filed, both sides engage in the legal process called discovery. Each party is allowed to investigate what it is the other side is going to say if the case goes to trial. ICBC will be permitted access to your medical and work history, including your income records. You may have to testify at a discovery under oath and you may be required to submit to a medical examination by one or more physicians of ICBC's choosing. The defendant driver is also subject to discovery and will have to give sworn testimony about the accident.

Q: What is an examination for discovery? Will the other lawyer harass me?
A: An examination for discovery is when your lawyer asks the person who caused the accident questions under oath, and ICBC's lawyer asks you questions. It takes place in a boardroom at a court reporter's office or law office - not in a courtroom. The only people present are the lawyers, the parties to the lawsuit and the court reporter. By agreement, a spouse who was not injured may attend for moral support.

If the law does not require you to answer a certain question your lawyer will object to the question and instruct you to not answer it. He will object to questions on subjects that are not relevant to your claim for damages or that ask about privileged matters (confidential in law). There are several types of privilege.

Your lawyer will meet with you to help you prepare for the examination. If your sworn testimony contradicts the clinical notes and reports of your doctors and other treatment practitioners or your statements to the police and to ICBC after the accident, your credibility will be reduced; therefore, it is well worth your time to review these documents before your discovery.

Most ICBC lawyers are not rude or obnoxious at your discovery. In fact, many have learned from experience that they obtain many more admissions favourable to them from injured claimants by being very nice to them. The ICBC lawyer will ask you about:
- your state of health, your activities and your employment before the accident,
- the accident itself, and
- how you have progressed over time since the accident in terms of your pain, psychological state, limitations, activities, household chores and work,
- the steps you have taken to get better and the efforts you made,
- your present condition.

ICBC's lawyer may also ask you what percent you improved at various times since the accident. If you cannot answer such a question on a percentage basis, you do not have to do so; you may simply describe how you felt and what you have been able to do during various periods since the accident.

Q: What is discovery of documents?
A: You will provide your lawyer with all documents that may be relevant to your claim. Your lawyer's assistant will prepare a list of your documents and request a list of every relevant document that ICBC and the person who injured you may have. Both sides can claim "privilege" (confidentiality in law) on certain documents, and either side may challenge any claim of "privilege." The law on "privilege" is beyond the scope of this book.

We can obtain additional documents from ICBC by way of a Freedom of Information (FOI) request. Two examples of what we can obtain from an FOI request are:
- adjuster's notes of what your family doctor or physiotherapist said to the adjuster, and
- decisions on whether or not ICBC budgeted for video surveillance.

Q: Do I have to go to trial if I sue?
A: Most cases settle before the injured person goes to trial. When both sides are unable to reach a settlement, some cases proceed to trial. No one is required to proceed to trial, but may do so by choice. It is an injured person's choice whether he or she accepts ICBC's last offer before the trial or has the court decide the case. This decision is based on an assessment of the chances of recovering more than ICBC's final offer. It is also based on a number of personal factors, including one's willingness to have one's personal life discussed in detail in a courtroom.

You do not have to attend the trial unless you are testifying. If your doctor suggests that it would be detrimental for you to hear all the evidence about your problems, it may be in your best interests not to attend the trial at all except when you testify.

CHAPTER 22

SETTLEMENT NEGOTIATIONS

Q: When is the best time to try to settle my claim?
A: This depends upon what you mean by "the best time." Do you mean "when you will likely obtain the largest settlement" or "the earliest time that you will obtain a settlement that is marginally satisfactory at best"?

It also depends upon how serious your injuries are and whether you are financially desperate or stressed by the process. If you are in a very difficult position financially, or you find that dealing with ICBC is unduly stressful, you may feel a lot of pressure to settle as soon as possible. Try to resist this temptation. Wait to negotiate - at least until you've had your injuries for several months or until a medical specialist you trust is able to predict your long-term future. If you have ongoing problems or if there is a risk that you may develop post-traumatic arthritis, a specialist may not be able to confidently predict your long-term future for two to four years after your accident. (If you insist, the specialist may be able to give a more general prediction of your future at an earlier date.)

Injury lawyers have learned from experience that ICBC generally is not prepared to pay injured people top dollars to settle their claims until a few weeks, or even days, before their trial date. Therefore injury lawyers tend to wait until as close to the trial date as possible to negotiate most of their clients' claims. You - the client - are the boss, not your lawyer. If your need to resolve your claim early outweighs your desire to obtain the largest possible settlement, you may want to negotiate earlier. You are free to ask your lawyer to try to settle earlier than he might normally negotiate a claim such as yours.

Q: Do I have to settle my claim within two years of the date of the accident?
A: No, you do not have to settle your claim for damages within two years. In fact, most people with serious, long-term injuries do not settle their claims within two years. Within two years, however, you must initiate a law suit or your claim ceases to exist- -except if the injured person is under nineteen years of age or is mentally incompetent. I discuss this at the beginning of the Chapter 21.

Q: How does ICBC determine how much to offer a claimant for pain and suffering?
A: ICBC looks at the extent of "objective signs" of your injuries and limitations over time. These include:
* muscle spasms your doctors found over time,
* limitations in your range of motion over time,
* positive results on x-rays, CT scans, MRI's, bone scans, nerve conduction velocity testing, ENG (electromyography), EEG and other established scientific tests,
* the results of work capacity evaluations conducted by certified work capacity evaluators,
* Visible scars or deformities.

ICBC also considers what your credibility (or believability) would be if you took your case to court. This is based on a number of issues such as:

- Did video surveillance show you looking as disabled or less disabled than your treatment practitioners thought you were?
- Did interviews by an investigator of neighbours or employers or co-workers turn up anything positive or negative about you?
- Did your treatment practitioners comment negatively or positively about your desire and efforts to overcome your injuries?
- Did you present yourself to the adjuster as motivated and legitimate?
- Did you present yourself this way to ICBC's lawyer at your examination for discovery?
- Was your sworn testimony at your examination for discovery consistent with, or contradictory to, other evidence such as witness statements, your initial statement to ICBC and your medical records?
- Did the doctor to whom ICBC sent you comment negatively or positively on your condition, and how credible will he likely be in court compared to your own medical experts?

These factors will also influence how much ICBC will offer you for your financial losses such as loss of income.

If a claimant suffers a fairly minor injury, ICBC adjusters usually follow policy "guidelines" that define how they can settle the pain and suffering component of such claims.

In more serious claims, ICBC's adjusters will look at judges' written decisions regarding injuries similar to yours. This tells them what judges have previously awarded in such cases.

ICBC considers all the above factors to decide what a judge or jury may award you.

ICBC also considers the likelihood that you will take your case to court if it makes a low offer. Are you likely to accept it rather than go to court? Are you financially desperate? Do you appear unwilling to take any risk (a trial always involves some risk)? Do you appear averse to the stress and loss of privacy that a trial entails?

ICBC will also consider your lawyer's skill and track record.

Q: What is a mediation? Will it help me?
A: For centuries, lawyers have negotiated cases on behalf of their clients. In 1998, the British Columbia government passed the "Notice to Mediate Regulation." It gives injured people a valuable tool in their arsenal for negotiating certain cases. A good mediator can make a real difference in achieving a fair settlement.

After you have sued, and up to 77 days before your trial date, either ICBC's lawyer or your lawyer may deliver to the other side a form called a Notice to Mediate. The lawyers agree on an independent mediator in whom they both have confidence. They then set a date for the mediation. The cost of the mediation is borne equally by each side.

You may claim reimbursement of your share of this cost as part of your settlement or court award.

Seven days before the mediation, both sides must deliver a written mediation brief. You and your lawyer should meet to read and discuss the mediation briefs from both sides and thoroughly prepare for the mediation.

The mediation starts with both lawyers giving brief opening statements. Then both sides informally discuss the issues of the claim. The adjuster will often ask the injured person a number of questions to get a feeling for how the injured person would present in court. Often this is the first time the adjuster has met the injured person, as ICBC usually appoints a new adjuster after a claimant hires a lawyer. Until then, all the adjuster has seen is a lot of paper.

The next phase of the mediation is the exchange of an offer and then a series of counter-offers. Between each counter-offer, one of the two sides goes into a separate "breakout room." Then each side separately and confidentially discusses their position and negotiating strategy with their lawyer. Negotiations may continue over the next hour to several hours.

Most of the time, a settlement is successfully reached by the end of the mediation. If your case does not settle at the mediation, negotiations may continue at a later date. If the two sides cannot arrive at a settlement agreement, your case proceeds to trial.

Many less serious cases settle without mediation.

For further information about your claim and about Mr. Temple and his law firm, please visit www.icbcinjurylawyers.ca. If you have any questions for Mr. Temple that aren't answered in his book, please email him at ctemple@tntlawyers.ca.